A Note From Rick Renner

I am on a personal quest to see a "revival of the Bible" so people can establish their lives on a firm foundation that will stand strong and endure the test as end-time storm winds begin to intensify.

In order to experience a revival of the Bible in your personal life, it is important to take time each day to read, receive, and apply its truths to your life. James tells us that if we will continue in the perfect law of liberty — refusing to be forgetful hearers, but determined to be doers — we will be blessed in our ways. As you watch or listen to the programs in this series and work through this corresponding study guide, I trust you will search the Scriptures and allow the Holy Spirit to help you hear something new from God's Word that applies specifically to your life. I encourage you to be a doer of the Word He reveals to you. Whatever the cost, I assure you — it will be worth it.

> Thy words were found, and I did eat them;
> and thy word was unto me the joy and rejoicing of mine heart:
> for I am called by thy name, O Lord God of hosts.
> — Jeremiah 15:16

Your brother and friend in Jesus Christ,

Rick Renner

Encountering God's Powerful Presence in Worship
Steps To Enter God's Powerful Presence in Personal Worship

Copyright © 2022 by Rick Renner
P.O. Box 702040
Tulsa, OK 74170

Published by Rick Renner Ministries
www.renner.org

ISBN 13: 978-1-6675-0025-6

eBook ISBN 13: 978-1-6675-0026-3

How To Use This Study Guide

This five-lesson study guide corresponds to *"Encountering God's Powerful Presence in Worship" With Rick Renner* (**Renner TV**). Each lesson in this study guide covers a topic that is addressed during the program series, with questions and references supplied to draw you deeper into your own private study of the Scriptures on this subject.

To derive the most benefit from this study guide, consider the following:

First, watch or listen to the program prior to working through the corresponding lesson in this guide. (Programs can also be viewed at **renner.org** by clicking on the Media/Archive links.)

Second, take the time to look up the scriptures included in each lesson. Prayerfully consider their application to your own life.

Third, use a journal or notebook to make note of your answers to each lesson's Study Questions and Practical Application challenges.

Fourth, invest specific time in prayer and in the Word of God to consult with the Holy Spirit. Write down the scriptures or insights He reveals to you.

Finally, take action! Whatever the Lord tells you to do according to His Word, do it.

For added insights on this subject, it is recommended that you obtain Philip Renner's book, *Worship Without Limits: The Place of Supernatural Access to God's Presence and Power,* and Rick Renner's book *A Life Ablaze.* You may also select from Rick's other available resources by placing your order at **renner.org** or by calling 1-800-742-5593.

TOPIC

God's Powerful Presence in Personal Worship

SCRIPTURES

1. **John 4:23,24** — But the hour cometh, and now is, when the true wor-shippers shall worship the Father in spirit and in truth: for the Father seeketh such to worship him. God is a Spirit: and they that worship him must worship him in spirit and in truth.

GREEK WORDS

1. "worship" — προσκυνέω (*proskuneo*): to draw near and to blow intimate kisses in worship

SYNOPSIS

The five lessons in this study on *Encountering God's Powerful Presence in Worship* will focus on the following topics:

- God's Powerful Presence in Personal Worship
- God's Powerful Presence Is With Us Everywhere We Go
- God's Powerful Presence in New Testament Songs
- God's Powerful Presence in Psalms, Hymns, and Spiritual Songs
- God's Powerful Presence in Different Sounds and Styles

The emphasis of this lesson:

"…True worshippers shall worship the Father in spirit and in truth…" (John 4:23). Worship literally creates a channel, or conduit, through which the Spirit of God enters the atmosphere. To be true worship, it must come from *the heart*. This kind of worship causes God's divine presence to manifest, and everything is then subject to being changed supernaturally!

Before the revolution of 1917, Nicolay Yusupov had a magnificent collection of rare musical instruments. The majority of them were housed in St. Petersburg, Russia, in the music room of the Yusupov Palace. Today an organ is the only piece that remains from the original collection, which included a Stradivarius and all kinds of rare violins. After the revolution, the instruments were all nationalized and taken to a museum.

Concerts took place all the time in the music room of the Yusupov Palace. People went there to hear the finest music. And the Bible tells us God enjoys good music too. When we worship from our hearts and give our best, it attracts the presence of God — and where the presence of God is, the supernatural takes place.

What Happens When People Worship God From Their Hearts?

When the Body of Christ worships, it attracts the very presence of God. And when His presence comes, His glory, which is heavy with everything good, meets the needs of everyone in the place. When we worship God from our hearts and give Him our best, His presence fills the atmosphere. That's what happens when we *really* worship God! Psalm 22:3 says, "But thou art holy, O thou that inhabitest the praises of Israel." This tells us God loves our worship so much that He sits enthroned on the praises of His people.

If you want to bring the presence of God right into your situation, worship God, and He will come. Worship forms a channel, or a conduit, for the presence of God to flow into your situation, and, as a result, it shifts the atmosphere.

Genuine Experiences in Worship

In the program, Rick shared the following experiences:

> I want to tell you about my first experience with genuine worship. Denise and I grew up in the same denomination. The denomination that we grew up in was wonderful, and I'm so thankful we grew up in that denomination because they really taught us the Bible, and they taught us to respect spiritual authority. But, for me personally, I didn't understand worship. For example, in our service we didn't have a 'worship service,' we had a 'song service.'

We didn't have a 'praise and worship ministry,' we had a 'music program.' It was all about music. And by the way, the music was off the charts!

We had all kinds of choirs, youth choirs, and children's choirs. I was in choir from the time that I can remember. I'm very grateful for the music program that we had in our church. People learned to sing solos, and people learned to play different instruments.

But I never experienced worship until I attended a Kathryn Kuhlman meeting. I joined the choir, not because I wanted to be part of the choir, but because somebody told me that when you have a seat in the choir, you're closer to the stage and you can see the action take place right in front of you.

Well, I'd never been to a Kathryn Kuhlman meeting before, but I joined the choir and went to all the choir rehearsals, which were held at First Methodist Church in downtown Tulsa. And, finally, the day came for the big Kathryn Kuhlman miracle service, which was held on the campus of Oral Roberts University.

I got there and took my place in the big, big, I mean massive, choir and watched as the doors opened and people began flooding that auditorium. I was stunned. I mean, people were racing in to try to get a seat. And then they began to bring in all the people in wheelchairs, and stretchers, and people who came with doctors and nurses that were critically, *critically* ill. I'd never seen so many sick people gathered together in one place.

And then we began to sing songs. But then a moment came when we stopped singing hymns and the entire crowd began to sing the old song *Hallelujah,* and something happened. First of all, I'd never heard that many people sing that song, but they weren't just singing a song — it was like worship swept across that massive auditorium and it lifted me to a place that I had never been in my life.

And it's interesting that about that moment, Kathryn Kuhlman came on stage, and that's when the miracles began to take place. She was so smart. She knew to make the entrance when the presence of God had come, and she didn't come on stage until first a conduit had been formed for the presence of God to invade the auditorium.

When people began singing *Hallelujah*, I felt like it just lifted me to some place I'd never been in my life. I didn't even know I could be in such a place. It was the first time I'd ever experienced worship, and it literally shifted the atmosphere.

Singing in Tongues Brings God's Presence

Rick went on to share about a second experience with genuine worship: "The second time I experienced worship was when I attended a little Bible study in Sand Springs, Oklahoma, where I grew up. As I was sitting there, I felt so awkward because I was in a Spirit-filled environment and I hadn't been in many environments like that. Suddenly, everyone in the room joined hands, and they began to sing in tongues."

In the program, Rick then asked Denise, "Do you remember the first time you heard singing in tongues? I think it's the most beautiful thing that I've ever heard. In that moment, I felt like we had joined the realm of angels; it's like the spirit realm opened and, suddenly, God's presence filled that room."

Denise also related her first experience with worship. They were in a little church with about 18 people, and nobody focused on what you looked like or sounded like. The worship leader simply poured her heart out to Jesus. Denise was on the front row, and it wasn't long until she was on her face before the Lord. What she experienced on the floor that night, she had never experienced before in her life.

Denise explained, "It was as if I was touching eternity. Maybe you're saying, 'What does that mean?' Well, I can't explain it very well, but I know that's where we're going. We're going to spend eternity with Jesus in that realm, in that place of glory." What Denise described was more than a song service; it was a *worship* service.

When you look at the Old Testament, notice that when worship occurred in the temple, it formed a channel for the presence of God to come into that place. When His presence came, it so charged the atmosphere and became so heavy that the priests could not stand to minister. They collapsed under the weight of God's glory (*see* 2 Chronicles 5:14). This agrees with Psalm 22:3, which tells us God sits enthroned on the praises of His people. God is *attracted* to worship just like metal is attracted to a magnet.

When You Genuinely Worship — You Experience God

Recent studies show that a surprising number of Christian leaders do not grasp an understanding of what worship really is. It is also known that many adults who consistently go to church and worship services say they have not actually experienced God's presence. That means for these people, real worship did not occur. Their church simply had a song service.

Many people also say that worship is something they do for their own benefit, in other words, they do it to feel good or to find relief. But worship is not for *us* — worship is for *God*! And when you create that conduit for His presence, God comes.

Pastor and author, David Jeremiah said, "If you don't worship, you'll never experience God." That's the truth; worship really is *that* vital. But what *is* worship and what *isn't* worship? First of all, worship is not just about music. Although music helps, you don't have to have music to worship. You can worship by yourself sitting in your living room.

In the program, Rick shared:

> When I went to that little Bible study in Sand Springs, there was no music at all. We just began to sing in tongues, and it took us into a place of amazing worship. ...I'll give you another example: Denise and I live in Moscow, Russia. Right in the very heart of Moscow is the world-renowned Bolshoi Theater. And because Denise is trained operatically, from time to time she and I attend events at the Bolshoi Theater where you [can] see the finest ballet on the planet, you can hear the best opera that can be heard, and the orchestra pit is filled with the best players that exist in the world. That's just the Bolshoi Theater.
>
> When you sit in your chair in the Bolshoi Theater, first of all, it's such an honor to be there because it's such a prestigious place. But to say that it leaves you *speechless* would be an understatement. In fact, often I'm sitting next to Denise and someone will begin to sing an aria, and Denise will reach over and begin squeezing my leg so hard. She's so excited and so intense, I think, *Please quit squeezing my leg*, but it's because she's so blessed by what she's hearing!

Or the chorus begins to sing, or suddenly dancers come on stage. There's nothing like watching Russian ballet! I mean, the men can leap like nobody else in the world. But you know what, as good as the music is, and as good as the instrumentalists and the dancers are, *it doesn't bring the presence of God.* The Bolshoi Theater, which I love, is a cathedral to human achievement.

Rick concluded, unfortunately, that's what a lot of churches have become. They have the very best songs — in fact, their songs are nearly choreographed, with every movement planned. Certainly, we need to be the best we can be because we're serving the Lord, but if we're giving *only* our fingers, head, voice, and talent — it is *not* worship; it's just really good music. And good music on its own does not constitute the kind of worship that charges the atmosphere with the powerful presence of God.

True Worship Comes From the Heart

Music by itself does not bring the presence of God. It can assist that process, but to really be worship, it has to involve *the heart.* True worship comes from *the heart,* and it literally attracts the presence of God.

Jesus referred to worship from the heart when He said, "But the hour cometh, and now is, when the true worshippers shall worship the Father in spirit and in truth: for the Father seeketh such to worship him. God is a Spirit: and they that worship him must worship him in spirit and in truth" (John 4:23,24).

The words "worship" and "worshipper" come from the same Greek word, *proskuneo,* which is mentioned five times in John 4:23 and 24. Jesus is clearly making a point! The Greek word *proskuneo,* comes from two words, *pros* and *kuneo.* The first word, *pros,* means *to draw as near as you can,* which tells us that worship is not just singing a song; it's the act of *drawing near.* The second word, *kuneo,* is a Greek word which means *to kiss* or *to blow kisses.*

When you compound the two words together, the word "worship" means *to draw near and to blow intimate kisses in worship.* It pictures one who has drawn near to the Lord, and with his heart, with his spirit, with his entire being, he is being intimate with God.

In the program, Rick related, "We grew up singing songs like, '*Blessed assurance,* Jesus is mine! Oh, what a foretaste of glory divine. Heir of

Salvation, purchase of God, born of His Spirit, washed in His blood...."[1] We could have worshiped with that song, but I wasn't looking at the words; I was looking at the *notes*. I wanted to hit every note just right because we had a music program in our church. I missed the meaning in those words."

Worship Is All About Him!

Denise shared, "Worship is not about music; it's about a Person. It's about the Person that you adore, the Person who saved you, the Person whom you have a relationship with. It's all about Him, and when you make it all about Him, then He comes with His mighty presence and He brings you what you need — which is Him."

Notice David's attitude toward worship in Psalm 63:1. He said, "O God, thou art my God; early will I seek thee: my soul thirsteth for thee, my flesh longeth for thee...." You see, worship is all about *seeking* God! David said, "...My soul thirsteth for thee..." It's about being thirsty! Have you ever been thirsty? How thirsty are you for Him? David went on to say, "...My flesh longeth for thee...." Do you have that kind of heart? Do you long for Him? If you have a heart like that, it is worship to God.

The word "worship," the Greek word *proskuneo*, means to draw near with your whole heart. It doesn't mean to just blurt out notes and music. And Jesus says God is *seeking* such to worship Him. When we enter into that place, God sits on our praises — He sits on our worship — and like metal is attracted to a magnet, the presence of God comes, and when His presence comes, *everything* changes.

In our next lesson, we're going to see that we can worship everywhere we go. Do you know why? Because we are the temple of the Holy Spirit. The Holy Spirit lives in us; we are a walking cathedral, which means we can worship personally *anywhere* we are.

STUDY QUESTIONS

Study to shew thyself approved unto God, a workman that needeth not to be ashamed, rightly dividing the word of truth.
— 2 Timothy 2:15

The ideas for most of the books Rick has written came either when he was in a worship service or praying in tongues. Why? Because when you're worshiping or praying in tongues, it shifts the atmosphere, and you're able to *see* things you couldn't see before. You're able to *hear* things that you couldn't hear before. In God's presence, He reveals His divine will for *you*!

1. Rick described the fabulous music heard in the Bolshoi Theater. Although the natural talent represented there is almost beyond description, it doesn't have the same result as anointed worship. As much as the human talent on that stage enthralls the audience, the presence of God is not ushered in through those performances. Why doesn't beautiful music alone usher in God's presence? Is true worship based on talent? If someone is anointed by God as a musician, can their musical talent enhance worship?

2. Notice the extreme value of the ministry of music. In Second Kings 3:15, how was an anointed musician's gift used? In Second Chronicles 5:13 and 14, how did God respond when they lifted up their voices with the trumpets, cymbals, and instruments of music and praised the Lord?

3. God's powerful presence manifests when you worship Him — not only in an assembly of believers, but also by yourself! Worship brings the presence of God to an individual or congregation. As a child of God, you can worship both privately and corporately, and the presence of God will come. What are some things you can do to enhance your private time of worship?

PRACTICAL APPLICATION

But be ye doers of the word, and not hearers only,
deceiving your own selves.
—James 1:22

1. God does amazing things when you worship Him: He heals, restores, delivers, gives direction and more! In fact, the Bible tells us, "...Times of refreshing shall come from the presence of the Lord" (Acts 3:19). What has God done in your life during precious times of worship? Write them down and thank God for them!

2. God wants to take you into new realms of worship. He wants to invade the very atmosphere of your home with His holy presence. Open the door for that to happen now, and you will be amazed at the depths of Him you experience. Take time today to press into His pres-

ence and rejoice in His goodness. Meditate on Psalm 136:1, Psalm 147:1, and Psalm 66:2 (*AMPC*).

3. Have you ever just spontaneously lifted praise in your heart to God? Imagine the delight of the Father hearing the sound of your voice as your heartfelt worship rises up to Him. Let His Word be the theme of your song (*see* Psalm 119:54).

4. In the program, Rick mentioned that when he reads his Bible, he takes a moment to sing praises to the Lord. Is there a verse in God's Word that is resonating in your heart at this time? During your personal time alone with God, take a moment to *sing* that scripture to Him as an act of worship!

---

[1] Fanny Crosby, "Blessed Assurance," Public Domain.

TOPIC

God's Powerful Presence Is With Us Everywhere We Go

SCRIPTURES

1. **1 Corinthians 6:19** — What? know ye not that your body is the temple of the Holy Ghost....

2. **Matthew 26:30** — And when they had sung an hymn, they went out into the mount of Olives.

3. **Mark 14:26** (*NKJV*) — And when they had sung a hymn, they went out to the Mount of Olives.

4. **Acts 2:46,47** — And they, continuing daily with one accord in the temple, and breaking bread from house to house, did eat their meat with gladness and singleness of heart, praising God, and having favour with all the people....

5. **Acts 16:25** — ...Sang praises unto God....

GREEK WORDS

1. "temple" — ναός (*naos*): a temple or a highly decorated shrine with vaulted ceilings, marble, granite, gold, silver, and highly decorated ornamentation

SYNOPSIS

The ballroom of the Yusupov Palace in St. Petersburg, Russia, is magnificent. The Yusupovs were distant relatives of the Czar, and it was not unusual for the Romanovs themselves to come to this spectacular palace. The chandelier in the ballroom was often referred to as the "diamond chandelier" because all its crystals were cut the same way a diamond is cut.

The music in that beautiful ballroom was simply breathtaking. And people enjoyed the music without seeing the musicians because a grill covered the area where the orchestra played. People danced, not only dressed in beautiful gowns and gorgeous clothes, but were also adorned with exquisite jewelry.

All of this took place in the ballroom for the pleasure of *people*. If all of that was done for the pleasure of man, think of how much more important it is that we worship God with the highest level of excellence musically, and with *all* of our heart. Jesus said that is what *God* is seeking — worshipers who worship Him in spirit and in truth.

The emphasis of this lesson:

When you were born again, the Holy Spirit came into your heart and gave life to your spirit. His work inside you was so glorious that when it was finished, He moved in, settled down, and took up residency inside your heart. You became *His* temple. You are a walking cathedral, and you take God with you wherever you go! You can launch into worship anytime, and anywhere.

True Worship Forms a Channel That Brings the Spirit of God Into the Very Atmosphere

As we learned in our last lesson, there's a vast difference between a "song service" and true worship. Some churches have phenomenal music programs, yet no revelation of worship. They're more concerned about singing each note correctly than they are about worshiping God from their heart.

You may sing beautiful songs in your church, but have you considered the truth contained within the very words you're singing? Or are you just caught up in following the notes correctly so you sound good? Look at the power contained in the words from the classic hymn, "Redeemed, How I Love to Proclaim It!" "Redeemed, how I love to proclaim it! Redeemed by the blood of the Lamb; redeemed through His infinite mercy, His child, forever I am. Redeemed, redeemed, redeemed by the blood of the Lamb; redeemed, how I love to proclaim it! His child, and forever I am...."[1]

Are you singing words filled with power, yet overlooking the very power in the words you're singing? Are the words just part of the "song service" rather than genuine worship? If you're more focused on singing the right notes than worshiping and you haven't grasped the power in the very words you are singing — that can change!

When you enter into true worship, it shifts the atmosphere, and brings the presence of God on the scene. Psalm 22:3 declares that God sits enthroned on the praises of His people. When you really worship from the heart, it's like metal attracted to a magnet — the presence of God comes. Worship literally forms a conduit that brings the Spirit of God into your space.

The manifested presence of God came when the Temple in Jerusalem was being dedicated (see 2 Chronicles 5:13,14). There was such an element of worship, that God's glory filled the temple, and it was so heavy that the priests could not even physically stand to minister. They collapsed under the presence of God.

Your Body Is the Temple of the Holy Spirit

In the center of Moscow, there is a huge Orthodox cathedral called the Cathedral of Christ the Savior. When you walk inside, it leaves you speechless. The decorations are phenomenal, and what is really amazing is that it was built in the last twenty years. It's filled with marble, granite, brass, gold, silver, and precious gems. Paintings illustrating the Gospel adorn the ceiling and surround you inside the cathedral.

In the First Century, there were also many pagan temples. One example is the Pantheon, located in the city of Rome. It's still standing, and you can visit it today. When you walk into the Pantheon, you walk into a real pagan temple from two thousand years ago that stands nearly exactly as it stood back then. It's embellished with marble and statues, and it was converted into a Catholic church, so it was never destroyed.

In First Corinthians 6:19, the apostle Paul wrote, "What? know ye not that your body is the temple of the Holy Ghost...." He began with the word "what." In essence, Paul was saying, "What? Do you not understand? Haven't you gotten it yet?" And then he added, "...know ye not...," meaning, *have you not comprehended*, or *have you not grasped yet*, that your body is the temple of the Holy Spirit? The word "body" is the Greek word *soma*, and it refers to *the physical body*.

The word "temple" is the Greek word *naos*, and it describes *a highly decorated shrine with vaulted ceilings, marble, granite, gold, silver, and highly decorated ornamentation.* That sounds just like Christ the Savior (in Moscow), or the Pantheon (in Rome), or any temple in the modern or ancient world that was highly embellished with gold, silver, precious stones, all kinds of marble, granite, and decorations. We're talking about something so magnificent that it nearly leaves you speechless. That's the word used here to describe y*our body*.

We need to treat our bodies better. First Corinthians 6:19 says your physical body is the temple of the Holy Spirit. And Paul went on to say, "...Which you have of God...." God gave us the Holy Spirit, and now He lives *in* us.

You Can Worship God Anywhere You Go

In the program, Rick related, "When I was a kid, I loved to play like we were pirates looking for buried treasure. We always made a treasure map and put an 'X' on it. Well, hey! There really is a buried treasure, and it's inside us! 'X' marks the spot." We have this treasure in us, and God has made a *naos*, or a temple, inside us so magnificent that He said, "You know what, I really like that! I think I'm going to move in there." That's what happened to us in the new birth!

That is so exciting because we were spiritually dead, but in the new birth God quickened us, made us alive in Christ, and recreated us internally. If you have a bad self-image, you need a revelation of what you have on the inside of you because it will change what you think about yourself. You are a walking cathedral, and you take God with you *everywhere* you go.

And this leads us to the subject of worship. You can worship anywhere you go because you are a mobile sanctuary. It's also good to be in the house of the Lord and worship with other believers — in fact, something special happens when you worship with others! When you and another believers worship together, you bring *your* portion of Christ and they bring *their* portion of Christ. And when the two of you come together, you have a double portion of Christ as you worship. Likewise, if you worship with ten, twenty, or fifty others, all those different portions of Christ come together and provide a *corporate* supply of Christ, and His unlimited power fills the room.

When you begin to worship with other believers, you form a conduit through which the presence of God comes. And as the presence of God within your heart is released, the atmosphere shifts, miracles begin to take place, lives are changed, and revelation is unlocked. You begin to see things you were never able to see before simply because you are in an atmosphere of worship and God's presence fills the room.

Worship literally ushers in God's presence, and one of the greatest things you can have in your life is the presence of God. The word "worship" — the Greek word *proskuneo* — means *to draw near and to blow intimate kisses in worship*. It pictures drawing *as near as possible* to get into an intimate place where you begin to worship God with your whole heart. In that place, in the intimate presence of God, the supernatural begins to take place.

Jesus and His Disciples Were Worshipers

How do we know that Jesus and His disciples were worshipers? Because the Bible tells us in both Matthew 26:30 and Mark 14:26 (*NKJV*), which say, "And when they had sung a hymn, they went out to the Mount of Olives." Think about it! When Jesus came into the upper room and He washed the feet of His disciples, that was an intimate event.

Jesus was making a covenant with His disciples, and it was a tender, tender moment. How did they end it? They sang a hymn just before they went to the Mount of Olives where Jesus was going to be arrested. Following that, Jesus would also be beaten with stripes for our healing and die on the Cross for our peace and the forgiveness of sin.

But before all of that took place, *Jesus needed a profound experience with God*, and He and the disciples began to worship. We know that Jesus and His disciples were worshipers because singing a hymn together was the final thing they did before going to the Mount of Olives.

Hebrews 2:12 says, "...In the midst of the church will I sing praise unto thee." When we worship, Jesus joins us because even He is a worshiper who loves to worship the Father in spirit and in truth. This pattern of worship was imparted from Jesus to the apostles, and that's why we see the early believers regularly not only fellowshipping and taking communion, but also praising God together.

"And they, continuing daily with one accord in the temple, and breaking bread from house to house, did eat their meat with gladness and singleness of heart, praising God, and having favour with all the people. And the Lord added to the church daily such as should be saved" (Acts 2:46,47). Notice it says they were "praising God," and what happened right after that? The Bible tells us there was a supernatural invasion of God's presence, and thousands upon thousands of people were saved. Signs, wonders, and miracles started to happen in the city of Jerusalem. Glorious things occurred in the Early Church in connection with the atmosphere of worship.

Worship God in the Midst of Trouble and His Power Will Come on the Scene!

The Early Church saw God's presence bring healing, favor, and more. When a crowd of sick people couldn't all get to Peter, they were laid on the street across from him and were healed when his shadow fell upon them (*see* Acts 5:15,16)!

Another example in the Bible was when Paul and Silas were arrested for preaching the Gospel, and they were put into prison. In fact, they were in the deepest, darkest part of the dungeon. They knew, *If we don't do something, we're in trouble.* What did they do? After Paul and Silas were beaten and imprisoned, they prayed and "…sang praises unto God…" (Acts 16:25). They did not have a "song service" where every note had to be exact. They simply praised God wholeheartedly, and quite loudly! Acts 16:25 declares Paul and Silas prayed and sang praises unto God "…and the prisoners heard them."

When you are in serious trouble, you do more than sing notes. Paul and Silas were *proskuneo*; they were drawing near to God. They needed God's presence to invade that prison. They didn't hide or tone down their praise. They expressed their faith in God with fervency and expectancy. They were so loud, the other prisoners heard every word of their praise!

We read in Acts 16:26, "And suddenly there was a great earthquake, so that the foundations of the prison were shaken: and immediately all the doors were opened, and every one's bands were loosed." In their worship, Paul and Silas formed such a channel, such a conduit, that God's presence came into the prison and shook its very foundations.

The presence of God broke off their chains, miraculously and caused the prison doors to swing wide open, and the jailer and his entire family got saved and gave birth to the church in the city of Philippi. All of that was the result of the worship that took place in that prison. Think of what would have been missed if Paul and Silas had not chosen to worship in the prison!

Paul and Silas were in a desperate situation, and out of that place they sought the Lord. We have the promise that if we draw near to God, He will draw near to us. And He is the One who has all the answers and all the power to meet every need!

"Draw near to God, and he will draw near to you…" (James 4:8 *ESV*). That's the promise! When we worship God, we draw near to Him and seek after Him like the psalmist David did (*see* Psalm 63:1-3). We hunger and thirst after Him because when *God* comes, *everything* shifts.

Worship God With Your Voice and From Your Heart

Sometimes when talking about worship people say, "I'm not very musically skilled." But in the verses we've looked at in this lesson, there has not been a single mention of a musical instrument. All they had were their *hearts* and their *voices* — and that's *all* you need to worship God (*see* Matthew 26:30, Mark 14:26, and Acts 16:25).

Today, you can go online and listen to all kinds of worship music that can help you form that channel for God's power to come into any difficult place in your life. If you don't like what's going on in your house, then worship, worship, worship! You will encounter God's powerful presence in your times of personal worship, and He will come right into your house.

You house the very presence of God. What is inside you is more ornate than any cathedral made by man. What is inside you is so wonderful that God said, "I'm going to move in right here!" You can worship when you read your Bible, you can worship as you get ready for your day, you can worship when you walk, you can worship when you're in the car, and you can worship everywhere you go because you are the temple of the Holy Ghost, which you have of God. You're a walking cathedral!

STUDY QUESTIONS

Study to shew thyself approved unto God, a workman that needeth
not to be ashamed, rightly dividing the word of truth.
— 2 Timothy 2:15

1. When you sincerely draw near to God, and worship Him from your heart, you will encounter His powerful presence. No matter the situation you may be facing, the presence of God will come to shift the environment and change things in your life as you worship Him. Praise Him as an act of faith today (*see* John 9:38, Ephesians 5:20, and Psalm 79:13).

2. Notice in Acts 16:25 that Paul and Silas did two things: they prayed *and* sang praises unto God. Too many Christians simply pray and stop there. But the victory came when Paul and Silas were praising God! Notice how giving glory to God is seen combined with prayer throughout the Bible. Read Philippians 4:6 and Second Chronicles 20:4-24.

3. In moments when authentic worship transpires in a room full of united believers, the portion of Christ each person carries is released to produce a powerful, combined supply of His presence. When such worship occurs, God literally enters into the midst of it. What has God done in your life during times of corporate worship? Consider Psalm 35:18 and Psalm 63:1-4.

PRACTICAL APPLICATION

But be ye doers of the word, and not hearers only,
deceiving your own selves.
— James 1:22

1. How do you draw strength from God when you need it most? Before going to the Mount of Olives, Jesus needed a profound experience with God, and He and the disciples began to worship. Singing a hymn with His disciples was the final thing Jesus did before going to the Mount of Olives. Think of the strength He drew from that moment of corporate praise with those He loved most. Can you imagine how much He pressed into God's presence while singing that hymn? What are some worship songs you can sing when you are faced with challenges? The next time you face difficulties, remember

that Jesus worshiped God before going to the Cross, and take time to worship Him. You'll be amazed at how it strengthens you!

2. If churches don't take the time to worship until God's presence fills the room, they will miss a lot of things God wants to do. But when God's people come with sincere hearts of worship and His presence invades the room, supernatural things begin to happen! What can you do to enhance corporate worship in your church? Whether you are on the worship team or not, can your one genuine heart of worship impact the others present?

3. When the circumstances of life bombard you, lift your eyes above the storm and draw near to God in worship. He will invade the situations that trouble you most. Read Psalm 119:62 and Psalm 42:5, and then take some time to worship Him.

---

[1] Fanny Crosby, "Redeemed, How I Love to Proclaim It!" Public Domain.

LESSON 3

TOPIC

God's Powerful Presence in New Testament Songs

SCRIPTURES

1. **Ephesians 5:14** — Wherefore he saith, Awake thou that sleepest, and arise from the dead, and Christ shall give thee light.

2. **Colossians 1:15-20** — Who is the image of the invisible God, the firstborn of every creature: For by him were all things created, that are in heaven, and that are in earth, visible and invisible, whether they be thrones, or dominions, or principalities, or powers: all things were created by him, and for him: And he is before all things, and by him all things consist. And he is the head of the body, the church: who is the beginning, the firstborn from the dead; that in all things he might have the preeminence. For it pleased the Father that in him should all

fulness dwell; and, having made peace through the blood of his cross, by him to reconcile all things unto himself; by him, I say, whether they be things in earth, or things in heaven.

3. **Philippians 2:9,10** — Wherefore God also hath highly exalted him, and given him a name which is above every name: That at the name of Jesus every knee should bow, of things in heaven, and things in earth, and things under the earth.

4. **2 Timothy 2:11-13** — …For if we be dead with him, we shall also live with him: If we suffer, we shall also reign with him: if we deny him, he also will deny us: If we believe not, yet he abideth faithful: he cannot deny himself.

GREEK WORDS

There are no Greek words in this lesson.

SYNOPSIS

The Yusupov Palace in St. Petersburg, Russia, was the Yusupov family's home for five generations. It's remarkable that it was not destroyed during the Bolshevik Revolution. If you peeked into its ballroom before the revolution, you would have seen it filled with people dancing to the accompaniment of the most beautiful music. Live musicians sat behind a grill where they weren't seen but could be heard in both the ballroom and the Great White Banquet Room adjacent to it.

The embellishments in the ballroom of the Yusupov Palace are simply spectacular: The gold, the ornamentation on the ceiling, the chandelier, and more. But *you* are even more amazing — *you* are the temple of the Holy Spirit!

The emphasis of this lesson:

Early believers didn't just sing worship songs that made them feel good. Their songs called for consecration and commitment and mirrored the messages that were being preached at the time. While many people forget the words of a sermon, they remember a message set to music and take it everywhere they go, making worship songs vital to both the Early Church and believers today.

In First Corinthians 6:19, the apostle Paul wrote, "What? know ye not that your body is the temple of the Holy Ghost which is in you...." The word "temple" is the Greek word *naos*, and it describes *a highly decorated shrine*. This verse tells us that if your eyes were opened and you could see *inside* yourself, you would find that what is *in* you is far greater than anything you see in the Yusupov Palace or any other man-made structure. You are embellished by God *inwardly*. In fact, you are a walking sanctuary.

You can worship God anywhere and at any moment because you take Him with you everywhere you go. While it's wonderful to go to church and worship with other believers, you don't have to wait until you are inside the church building to worship!

Worship Forms a Channel Through Which God's Manifested Glory Comes

In the program, Rick related the following about his experience with worship:

> God doesn't want us just to have a song service [in our church]. God wants us to *encounter His powerful presence* in worship. How in the world did we not understand that when we were growing up?
>
> ...I think about the words we used to sing: "...*Redeemed through His infinite mercy, His child, and forever, I am....*"[1] And you know, today I can sing that in my private time...when I'm reading my Bible and worshiping. But when I was young, I was just singing notes. I didn't even listen to what we were saying.... Personally, I did not understand worship. Maybe other people did; I did not.
>
> I never really encountered worship until I went to a Kathryn Kuhlman meeting. ...When people began to worship and sing the song *Halleluiah*, I thought, *What is happening? I've never felt anything like this!* And that was the first time I understood worship forms a conduit that brings the presence of God and shifts *everything* in the atmosphere.

Rick shared that when he first met Denise they were attending a small church at the university where they went to school. They didn't have many musical instruments (only a guitar), but their *hearts* were fully involved as they worshiped. As a result, God's presence came into those meetings, and they saw miracles, signs, and wonders! His powerful presence unleashed the gifts of the Holy Spirit!

Many churches have good music programs, but they don't understand worship. When you worship God from your heart, you *encounter* His presence and everything in the atmosphere changes. Psalm 22:3 declares that God inhabits, or sits enthroned upon, the praises of His people. And just like metal is attracted to a magnet, when you begin to worship, it attracts the presence of God.

Worship forms a channel through which God's manifested glory comes. And when His glory comes into the place, *everything* changes. Mysteries are unlocked, revelation is revealed, and people get healed! All of that *and more* happens when God's presence comes.

God's Presence Released Through New Testament Songs

Have you ever wondered what kind of songs were sung in the early days of the New Testament? Scholars speculate that there may be as many as thirty songs recorded in the New Testament, and together they are called hymnic literature.

Hymnic literature refers to any song that was sung in the Early Church and incorporated into the books of the New Testament. For example, the apostle Paul wrote to the church of Ephesus, trying to make a point, and suddenly, it's as if he said, "I know how to make this point! It's like the song you sing in your church." And he injected the words to a song they were singing in Ephesus into the letter he was writing.

In Paul's letter to the Colossians, we also find hymnic literature. Paul was writing about the deity of Jesus, and suddenly, he injected the words of a song into the letter. It's as though he said, again, "I know how to make my point. I will quote the words to a song you sing in your church."

Paul did the very same thing in the book of Philippians too. What's so powerful about this is that if you look at the songs which were sung in these churches, then you can understand what was being preached in the churches.

You May Forget Sermons, But Songs Stay With You!

How many sermons do you remember from your childhood? Probably not many. How many songs do you remember from growing up? Most likely, more than one. That's because songs stay with you. If you hear a message, you may forget it, but most people remember songs.

The songwriters in the First Century understood the power of taking sermons and putting them to music. From the hymnic literature we have, it looks like the leadership of the Early Church said, "This message is so important that I want you songwriters to put it to music so people can take it home and sing it." Think of the revelation that came into their hearts as they would sing the messages they heard over and over!

In the program, Rick shared, "Several years ago, I said to the songwriters in our church in Moscow, 'These messages are so important that I want you to take what I'm preaching and put it into song so people can take my messages home and sing them — because *people don't forget what they sing.*'"

HYMNIC LITERATURE
Example One — Ephesians

There are many examples of hymnic literature, and the first one we will look at in the New Testament is found in Ephesians 5:14, which says, "Wherefore he saith, Awake thou that sleepest, and arise from the dead, and Christ shall give thee light."

This was part of a song — that makes it hymnic literature. It was a worship song they were singing in Ephesus, and Paul put it right into the text of his letter to the Ephesians.

HYMNIC LITERATURE
Example Two — Colossians

Another example of hymnic literature is found in the book of Colossians. This text speaks of Jesus and the deity of Christ: "Who is the image of the invisible God, the firstborn of every creature: For by him were all things created, that are in heaven, and that are in earth, visible and invisible, whether they be thrones, or dominions, or principalities, or powers: all things were created by him, and for him: And he is before all things, and by him all things consist.

"And he is the head of the body, the church: who is the beginning, the firstborn from the dead; that in all things he might have the preeminence. For it pleased the Father that in him should all fulness dwell; And, having made peace through the blood of his cross, by him to reconcile all things unto himself; by him, I say, whether they be things in earth, or things in heaven" (Colossians 1:15-20).

That's hymnic literature, and that's what the believers at Colossae were singing. If you sing the powerful words contained in Colossians 1:15-20, the power of God will be released in your life, and the presence of God will permeate the atmosphere around you!

The Colossians were dealing with some serious issues, and the apostle Paul reminded them that *Christ* was to be their focus. He said in essence, "Let me remind you, like the song you're singing in your church…." Paul took the hymnic literature — the lyrics to a song they were singing — and injected them right into the text.

HYMNIC LITERATURE
Example Three — Philippians

Let's look at a third example of hymnic literature: "Wherefore God also hath highly exalted him, and given him a name which is above every name: That at the name of Jesus every knee should bow, of things in heaven, and things in earth, and things under the earth" (Philippians 2:9,10). When you say those things out loud, it's an exhortation to your own soul, and it brings the powerful presence of God!

Philippians 2:9 and 10 quote what believers were singing in the church of Philippi. And who knows, it may have been popular in *all* the churches. It was popular enough that when Paul was writing his letter he thought to say, "I know how to make my point. It's like the song you are singing in your church." And he began to quote it.

Notice that Philippians 2:9 and 10 is a sermon in itself. If God has highly exalted Him and has given Him a name which is above every single name, then there's your healing! His name is above *every* sickness, including leukemia, blindness, and cancer. His name is above *every* name.

Throughout Paul's writings you'll often see hymnic literature. That tells us something else — *Paul* knew those songs! Certainly, he knew them. He walked everywhere in his ministry, he spent time on ships by himself, and he spent time alone in prison. Paul was a man who knew and sang these songs because they were revelation to him.

HYMNIC LITERATURE
Example Four — Second Timothy

There is a fourth example of hymnic literature, and it's found in Second Timothy. The apostle Paul wrote to Timothy, who was the pastor of the church in Ephesus, about being faithful and sticking with his commitment to the end regardless of the price that had to be paid. Then Paul quoted hymnic literature. It's almost like he said, "Oh, I know how to make the point. Let me quote the words to the song that you are singing in your church."

"…For if we be dead with him, we shall also live with him: If we suffer, we shall also reign with him: if we deny him, he also will deny us: If we believe not, yet he abideth faithful: he cannot deny himself" (2 Timothy 2:11-13).

These are not just words that make you feel good and pacified. These are *challenging* words that have to do with consecration and commitment. And these songs mirrored what was being preached in the church. What kind of a people would it take to sing, "If we be dead with Him we shall also live with Him?" They were singing that, and they went on to sing, "If we suffer, we shall also reign with him: if we deny him, he also will deny us: If we believe not, yet he abideth faithful: he cannot deny himself."

These believers were taking the message home and singing it. What a way to get revelation into your heart! *Sing* it into your heart! They formed a conduit, or a channel, through which God's powerful presence could come.

In Ephesus, they didn't preach about how to improve your personality, they preached about how to endure until the end and stay committed to Christ. That's what they sang, which means they saw themselves as an advancing army. They stirred themselves up to be faithful to the end regardless of what was required. And they sang and sang until they got that revelation down on the inside of them.

It's Time To Go to New Places in Worship

Through singing those songs, the believers in Ephesus released Gods' powerful presence — not only at church, but also in their home groups, their kitchens, as they were walking along the streets, and more.

In the program, Rick shared that when he and Denise got married they sang and sang. They worshiped God because they wanted God's presence to be in the middle of their marriage. When you worship God, He gets in the middle of everything that you're doing. You don't have to wait until you get to church. You are a walking cathedral, and you can worship everywhere you go.

In the next lesson, we will see God's powerful presence in psalms, hymns, and spiritual songs. If you can sing a psalm, a hymn, or a spiritual song *from the heart*, you can form a channel for God's presence to come. And when God's presence comes, demons flee, revelation is unlocked, and the atmosphere changes. All of that happens when you enter into worship because God's presence permeates the atmosphere.

STUDY QUESTIONS

Study to shew thyself approved unto God, a workman that needeth not to be ashamed, rightly dividing the word of truth.
— 2 Timothy 2:15

1. Read Psalm 9:1 and 2, Psalm 57:7, Psalm 86:12, and Psalm 111:1. What do they tell us about the posture of our heart during worship?

2. Read Psalm 8:1 and 2, Psalm 18:46-49, and Second Chronicles 20:21 and 22. What do these verses tell us about God as our deliverer?

3. Read Psalm 27:4-6, Psalm 18:1-3, Psalm 13:6, Psalm 16:7, and Psalm 117:2. What do these passages tell us about why we should worship God?

4. Notice the words "I will" in the following verses: Psalm 69:30 and Psalm 145:2 and 5. What should you do when things are so difficult that you really don't *feel* like worshiping God?

PRACTICAL APPLICATION

> But be ye doers of the word, and not hearers only,
> deceiving your own selves.
> — James 1:22

1. Your family may or may not be musically gifted, but the beautiful thing about worship is that it's of the *heart*. You don't have to be a professional singer or accomplished instrumentalist to simply lift *your* voice to the Lord in worship. The power of God can enter your space right now, shift the atmosphere, and change everything in your life in Jesus' name. Take some time to worship Him for who He is with a song of praise!

2. Do you remember what God said to you through your pastor at service this week? Why not follow the good example of the Early Church and take the portion of the message that resonated most in your heart and create a simple song out of it? As you sing it throughout the day, you'll help get those words of life from your head down into your heart and revelation will come as a result.

3. Read Psalm 103:1-5 and praise God for the many things this Psalm outlines that He has provided for you because of His great love. He has done so much for you, His beloved child!

---

[1] Fanny Crosby, "Redeemed, How I Love to Proclaim It!" Public Domain.

LESSON 4

TOPIC

God's Powerful Presence in Psalms, Hymns, and Spiritual Songs

SCRIPTURES

1. **Ephesians 5:19,20** — Speaking to yourselves in psalms and hymns and spiritual songs, singing and making melody in your heart to the

Lord; giving thanks always for all things unto God and the Father in the name of our Lord Jesus Christ.

2. **Colossians 3:16** (*NIV*) — ...Psalms, hymns, and songs from the Spirit, singing to God with gratitude in your hearts.

3. **Psalm 22:3** — But thou art holy, O thou that inhabitest the praises of Israel.

4. **Psalm 133:1-3** — Behold, how good and how pleasant it is for brethren to dwell together in unity! It is like the precious ointment upon the head, that ran down upon the beard, even Aaron's beard: that went down to the skirts of his garments; as the dew of Hermon, and as the dew that descended upon the mountains of Zion: for there the Lord commanded the blessing, even life for evermore.

GREEK WORDS

1. "psalms" — ψαλμός (*psalmos*): a song of praise

2. "hymns" — ὕμνος (*humnos*): a sacred composition designed to give glory to God

3. "spiritual songs" — ᾠδαῖς πνευματικαῖς (*odais pneumatikais*): songs in the Spirit; singing in the Spirit; singing in tongues

4. "singing" — ᾄδω (*ado*): to sing with the voice; describes expressive, vocal singing

5. "melody" — ψάλλω (*psallo*): to pluck the strings of a harp or bow; a heartfelt expression of music

6. "glory" — δόξα (*doxa*): something heavy or weighty; discernment, judgment, and splendor

SYNOPSIS

The Yusupov Palace in St. Petersburg, Russia, had a *real* home theater, which was quite different from today's in-home theaters. It was a *real* theater. The stage of this home theater hosted all kinds of performances: Opera, ballet, orchestral performances, and more. People applauded and celebrated everything that took place on that stage.

The apostle Paul wrote about praise and worship in Ephesians 5:19 and 20. He specifically mentioned psalms, hymns, and spiritual songs, which tells us that God enjoys it all! He likes a variety: Psalms, hymns, *and* spiritual songs. You may have one you like the most, but when it comes to praise and worship, God enjoys an assortment.

When you genuinely worship from your heart anywhere you are, you encounter God's powerful presence. When you worship, a conduit or channel is formed, through which the presence of God comes right into your atmosphere. And when His presence comes, it shifts the environment, everything changes, revelation is released, healing is received, and more.

The emphasis of this lesson:

When you make melody to the Lord with your heart, it may be expressed as a psalm, a hymn, or a spiritual song. God delights in it all so much that when you truly worship Him, He shows up with His presence — whether you are alone or assembled with other believers. His glory manifests, identifies your specific needs, and meets them. Hallelujah!

What Are Psalms, Hymns, and Spiritual Songs?

The apostle Paul wrote in Ephesians 5:19 and 20, "Speaking to yourselves in psalms and hymns and spiritual songs, singing and making melody in your heart to the Lord; giving thanks always for all things unto God and the Father in the name of our Lord Jesus Christ." In these verses, Paul mentioned psalms, hymns, and spiritual songs. In Greek, these are three very different words.

- "psalms" — the Greek word *psalmos,* **depicting** *a song of praise*

- "hymns" — the Greek word *humnos,* **describing** *a sacred composition designed to give glory to God*

- "spiritual songs" — the Greek phrase *odais pneumatikais,* **literally meaning** *songs in the Spirit; singing in the Spirit;* **or** *singing in tongues*

"...I will pray with the spirit, and I will also pray with the understanding. I will sing with the spirit, and I will also sing with the understanding" (1 Corinthians 14:15 *NKJV*). According to this verse, you can pray in your own natural language, and you can pray in the Spirit or pray in tongues. You can also sing in your own language as well as sing in the Spirit or in tongues.

In First Corinthians 14:17, Paul instructed that when you pray or sing in tongues "...you indeed give thanks well...." When you worship God by singing in tongues, you will indeed give thanks well!

When Paul said worship included "spiritual songs" in Ephesians 5:19, the Greek literally means *songs in the Spirit, singing in the Spirit,* or *singing in tongues.* Isn't that amazing? And then he went on to say, "...Singing and making melody in your heart to the Lord" (Ephesians 5:19). The word "singing" — the Greek word *ado* — means *to sing with the voice,* and it particularly describes *expressive vocal singing.*

How Special Is the Sound of Your Voice to God?

Singing is an attribute that belongs *only* to human beings. People think angels sing, and maybe they do, but the Bible never tells us that. It tells us about the four and twenty elders, which sing in heaven (*see* Revelation 4:10,11).

Regarding what the angels do, the Bible does say the angels "say" or the angels "declare," but there is no evidence in Scripture that angels sing. That may be quite a shock to some, but it also means singing is very special. When you sing, it's *a gift* that you give to the Lord.

When You Make Melody to the Lord With Your Heart the 'Instrument' You Play Is Your Heart Itself!

Ephesians 5:19 goes on to say, "...Singing and making melody in your heart to the Lord." The word "melody" is the Greek word *psallo,* which means *to pluck the strings of a harp or bow* and describes *a heartfelt expression of music.* But in this particular case, it's not describing instrumental music; it's talking about the melody, or song, in your heart.

Your spirit is like a harp, or a piano, and just like this verse says, you can pluck the strings of your heart in worship. When you make melody in your heart to the Lord, the instrument is not visible — it's with *your heart itself* that you sing to Him!

Taking into account the original Greek meaning, here is the *Renner Interpretive Version (RIV)* of Ephesians 5:19:

> **"You are to be continually speaking songs of praise, hymns, sacred compositions designed to give glory to God, and**

spiritual songs, which includes singing in the Spirit, along with heartfelt expressions in song that are plucked from the strings of your heart."

When you begin to worship God like that, it forms a conduit through which the presence of God comes and shifts the atmosphere. Paul also wrote about this in Colossians when he said you are to let the message of Christ dwell among you richly as you teach and admonish one another with all wisdom through "...psalms, hymns, and songs from the Spirit, singing to God with gratitude in your hearts" (Colossians 3:16 *NIV*).

Paul said we're to sing psalms, hymns, and songs from the Spirit. As we've seen, songs from the Spirit, or "spiritual songs," actually means songs *in* the Spirit, and it depicts *singing in tongues* or *singing in the Spirit*. In this verse, Paul was telling believers to use psalms, hymns, and songs from the Spirit to sing to God "with gratitude in your hearts" (Colossians 3:16).

How Does God Respond When You Worship From Your Heart?

The book of Psalms describes how God responds when you genuinely worship Him. "But thou art holy, O thou that inhabitest the praises of Israel" (Psalm 22:3). According to this verse, God inhabits the praise and the worship of His people.

The word "inhabitest" literally means *to sit enthroned on top of*. It pictures the presence of God coming down and sitting on top of an individual or a congregation who is worshiping. In essence, God is saying, "Oh, I like what they're doing so much I want to be a part of it!" And His presence comes and hovers right over that individual or right over that congregation. How powerful!

In the program, Denise shared, "Several years ago I was praying and singing with a new believer. And I said, 'We're going to praise the Lord.' So, I started praising the Lord. I was praising the Lord in English. And I told her 'Just speak from your heart how much you love the Lord. Just start praising Him.' So she praised Him in her language, [while] I praised Him in *my* language. The presence of God came, and she said, 'Well, something's happening, what is that?' I said, 'That is the presence of God.' She said, 'Oh, I like that. Let's keep doing that.'" That's what happens! God sits enthroned on top of our praise and our worship.

God's Presence Can Go Anywhere!

One example of God sitting enthroned on the praises of His people is found in Acts 16:25, when Paul and Silas were beaten and put in the deepest part of the prison. The Bible says they were singing and worshiping so loudly that all the prisoners could hear them, and suddenly, it was as if God said, "I'm going to go join them!" and His presence came into the very deepest part of that prison.

It doesn't matter where you are. If you begin to worship, it will open the floodgates of Heaven for the presence of God to come. God can go anywhere! When Paul and Silas were in jail praising God, He came with delivering and rescuing power that set them free!

In the program, Rick recounted, "I always think about Kathryn Kuhlman's meetings which had such an impact on my life. Sister Kuhlman really understood when to make an entrance. She wanted the power of God to be present before she ever came on stage to begin to minister. So the people began to worship and worship. You could nearly feel the entire auditorium being lifted up together into the presence of God when suddenly, God's power would begin to come into that auditorium.

"I can remember that even before Kathryn Kuhlman would speak, an announcer would come on stage and say, 'Miracles are already happening.' Why? Because they really weren't connected to Kathryn Kuhlman, she just understood how to create the *environment* where the power of God would come. And that's what happened in worship. God's glory came and sat on top of the congregation, and miracles began to happen."

'Glory' Describes the Weighty Presence of God Filled With Everything Good

When we talk about worship, we also talk about God's glory. The glory of God is the presence of God, and it manifests when you worship Him. In the Old Testament, the word "glory" describes *something heavy or weighty* and it pictures *a strong presence of God heavy with everything good*. God's glory is His weighty presence filled with everything good: revelation, provision, healing, and more!

We see an example of the glory of God in Second Chronicles 5:13 and 14, when the priests came into the temple to worship. As they were worshiping, what happened? God essentially said, "I'm going to join them," and His presence came. He sat enthroned upon them, and the glory was so heavy, the priests collapsed under the weight of it.

Have you ever been in a worship service where it felt like the atmosphere became heavy? That is evidence that the presence of God was in the room. When this happens you may not see His glory with your eyes, but when the atmosphere becomes heavy, reach out and receive what you need because the place is filled with *everything* good — it is filled with the glory of God!

God knows exactly what you need. When you open your heart and worship God, He comes with what you need. What did Paul and Silas need when they were imprisoned? They needed to be free from that jail, and when they sang praises unto God, He came and delivered them.

'Glory' Also Describes Discernment and Judgment

The word "glory" in the New Testament is a little different from the word "glory" in the Old Testament. In the New Testament, it's the Greek word *doxa*, which also describes *something heavy or weighty*; His weighty presence loaded with everything good. But the word *doxa* also carries the idea of *discernment*, *judgment*, and *splendor*.

When the glory of God comes into your room, or when the glory of God rests upon a congregation, the mind of God is in that glory. The glory of God hovering over the congregation *discerns* the needs in every single person. God *sees* the needs in every heart. The glory of God sees it all, and then begins to supernaturally distribute what is needed to every person.

When God's glory fills the room, if a person is in sin, the glory of God convicts them about it. If someone is depressed, the glory of God imparts encouragement. If a person is sick, they receive healing. If someone is bound, they receive freedom. That word "glory" carries the idea of discernment of your needs and distribution of what you need, and the glory manifests when the presence of God comes.

What Releases the Anointing in a Church?

Where there's unity among the brethren — in a church, between you and your spouse, or between you and another believer — something wonderful happens. Where there is unity, the Lord commands His blessing!

One of the most important passages in the Bible about the anointing says, "Behold, how good and how pleasant it is for brethren to dwell together in unity! It is like the precious ointment upon the head, that ran down upon the beard, even Aaron's beard: that went down to the skirts of his garments; as the dew of Hermon, and as the dew that descended upon the mountains of Zion: for there the Lord commanded the blessing, even life for evermore" (Psalm 133:1-3).

This is a picture of Aaron being anointed with oil. So much oil was poured on his head that it ran down his beard, came upon his garment, and ran down the pleats of his garments to the ground until Aaron was standing in a pool of anointing oil. That is so powerful! And when the Church gets into unity, God releases His Spirit until *we* stand in a pool of anointing.

What releases the anointing in the Church? Unity! Look again at verse 3: "As the dew of Hermon, and as the dew that descended upon the mountains of Zion: for there the Lord commanded the blessing, even life for evermore" (Psalm 133:3). Notice the Psalmist said the anointing that comes in the corporate atmosphere of worship is like "…the dew of Hermon, and as the dew that descended upon the mountains of Zion…." Let's talk about dew.

What Does Dew Have To Do With God's Anointing and His Glory?

In the program, Rick recounted:

> When I was a boy, I loved to go outside in the mornings because dew was everywhere. It's amazing that moisture is in the air all the time, but you can't *see* moisture. Sometimes you can *feel* it, but you cannot see moisture.
>
> There has to come a certain moment when the atmospheric conditions are met for the invisible moisture in the air to tangibly manifest and show up on the grass, or anything that's outside. There's an atmospheric moment when things change, and

suddenly what is invisible tangibly manifests and shows up, and *everything* is covered with droplets of water, which we call "dew."

It's like droplets of the anointing suddenly show up all over the auditorium [during worship], and that is why I always say there's nothing to be compared to a good worship service. In one worship service, more can be done than can be done in one hundred counseling sessions. And I believe in counseling!

The writer of this Psalm said the anointing is like dew. Think about it: the anointing is with us all the time, but you can't always see it. You can sense the presence of the anointing, but according to this passage there is a moment when unity comes (often during worship) when suddenly there is such a unified presence in the church, it's like the spiritual conditions are suddenly met in the very atmosphere.

When what is in the spirit realm and *invisible* suddenly shows up in the church, everybody gets touched. That's the corporate anointing! Everyone gets blessed! One person becomes joyous, another is healed, another is encouraged, another is strengthened, and another silently receives from the Lord.

When you're in a good worship service, and that conduit is created for the anointing to be released, suddenly the Spirit of God shows up, droplets of the anointing manifest all over the place, and now you're standing in a pool of anointing. When that happens, everyone gets changed and everyone gets touched. How powerful! We need to release our faith for that kind of anointing to show up in our *personal* worship times and in our *churches*.

You Can Worship Right Where You Are!

In the program, Rick shared, "Recently I've been worshiping every morning while I read my Bible because I understand that when I worship, it creates that conduit. Now, the Holy Spirit is there all the time, but we're talking about taking it out of the invisible realm and bringing it into the material, visible realm. I've been worshiping because I want to form that conduit for the presence of God to come to sit enthroned on top of me in my room…where I'm reading my Bible and praying and worshiping."

You can worship God right where you are! You can encounter God's powerful presence in worship. There's really no mystery to this. If you'll just begin to worship from your heart, it will throw open that portal for God's powerful presence to come, shift the atmosphere, and change everything in your life.

When you worship, you have an audience of One: God! And you encounter God's presence because He comes to join you. It's not just about singing songs, it's about creating a channel through which His presence comes, and you encounter *Him*. If you have a need in your life, begin to worship, and God's presence will manifest right where you are.

STUDY QUESTIONS

Study to shew thyself approved unto God, a workman that needeth not to be ashamed, rightly dividing the word of truth.
— 2 Timothy 2:15

1. Rick related the following in the program, "Every book I have written has been downloaded to me during times of worship or while praying in tongues. It's as if suddenly a barrier is removed and the Spirit of God communicates tasks, assignments, revelations, and truths to my spirit and mind. ...Suddenly I see what I was not able to see before!" Has God ever downloaded assignments, tasks, or wisdom to you in times of worship? What does Jeremiah 33:3 say we can expect in times of worship?

2. Psalm 16:11 says, "Thou wilt shew me the path of life: in thy presence is fulness of joy; at thy right hand there are pleasures for evermore." Do you need direction for your life? Consider First Corinthians 2:9 and 10, Romans 8:26 and 27, and Acts 13:2-4. What do these verses tell us about the Holy Spirit's role in our times of worship?

3. We are living at the end of the age, and we need to be in the corporate anointing now more than ever. Why is it so important to go to church and worship with other believers regularly? Consider Hebrews 2:12 and Hebrews 10:24 and 25.

4. If you haven't received the baptism in the Holy Spirit yet, now is a great time to receive. Read Mark 16:17; Acts 1:4,5,8; Acts 2:4,38,39; and Acts 10:45 and 46. Pray, "Lord, I ask you for the baptism in the Holy Spirit, and by faith I receive right now. Thank you for baptizing me in the Holy Spirit with the evidence of speaking with a new, supernatural prayer language. In Jesus' name. Amen." For more

information, see Rick's five-part series, *The Baptism in the Holy Spirit*, or call our prayer team at 1-800-742-5593.

PRACTICAL APPLICATION

> But be ye doers of the word, and not hearers only,
> deceiving your own selves.
> —James 1:22

1. When you sing and make melody to the Lord with your heart, the word "melody" refers to plucking the strings of a harp or bow. But the instrument you have inside you isn't a harp or bow — it's your *heart*! As you sing with earnest love to the Lord, it is like the sweetest melody to His ears. No wonder God sits or rests on a person who is truly worshiping Him from the heart! Take a few minutes to lift up a melody to the Lord from your heart now.

2. Once you are filled with the Holy Spirit with the evidence of speaking in tongues (*see* Acts 2:4), Ephesians 5:18 and 19 instructs you to be consistently "being filled" with the Spirit, speaking to yourself in psalms, hymns, and spiritual songs. Lift your hands to the Lord and receive a fresh infilling of the Holy Spirit. Consider Psalm 96:1, Psalm 98:1, and Psalm 149:1.

3. Starting today, make it your aim to include each of these three forms of worship during your time alone with God (*see* Colossians 3:16 and 1 Corinthians 14:26).

   • **Psalms — lift up a spontaneous song of praise**

   • **Hymns — praise Him with a sacred composition designed to give God glory**

   • **Spiritual songs — sing in the Spirit or sing in tongues**

TOPIC
God's Powerful Presence in Different Sounds and Styles

SCRIPTURES

1. **1 Corinthians 14:40** — Let all things be done decently and in order.
2. **John 4:23,24** — But the hour cometh, and now is, when the true worshippers shall worship the Father in spirit and in truth: for the Father seeketh such to worship him. God is a Spirit: and they that worship him must worship him in spirit and in truth.

GREEK WORDS

1. "decently" — εὐσχημόνως *(euschemonos)*: to do something honestly or to walk honestly; carries the idea of something done properly as opposed to being done improperly; has to do with intent and motivation more than outward action
2. "order" — τάξις *(taksis)*: something done in a fitting way or something done according to order

SYNOPSIS

The *heart* is what is most important when it comes to true worship. As time goes by, sounds and styles of worship change all over the world — but *the heart* remains the same, and that's what matters most.

God's presence will come anywhere when people truly worship Him. For example, Paul and Silas were in the deepest, darkest part of a prison in Philippi, but when they began to worship, the power and presence of God came into that deep, dark place (*see* Acts 16:25). The apostle John was in a cave on the isle of Patmos because of persecution, and the presence of God came into that cave (*see* Revelation 1:9,10).

The Bible tells us in First Corinthians 14:40 that in the house of God everything should be done "…decently and in order." But it seems everyone has a different opinion about what that means. What is decent and in order to one person might seem out of order to someone else.

The emphasis of this lesson:

Because cultures vary, all over the world as believers worship the sounds are different and the styles are different, but one thing is the same — *the heart*. And *the heart* of worship is what God is after!

There Are Diverse Styles and Sounds of Worship Worldwide

The worship of the New Testament Church most likely included musical elements from the Hebrew, Greek, and Roman cultures — depending on where the worship took place. People were being added to the Kingdom in various regions throughout the Roman world, Asia Minor (modern-day Turkey), Greece, Northern Africa, and other places in the Middle East. And because each was culturally different, it is likely that the styles, music, and expressions of worship varied from region to region and from culture to culture.

What is beautiful is that there is room for variation in styles of music when it comes to worshiping God. The most important thing is not that worship conforms to a certain style, but rather *that it comes from the heart.*

Today, we tend to get stuck on *our* favorite style of worship music. We may think it's right simply because it's all we know. But all over the world, there are many different blends and cultures in the Body of Christ. The sounds are different and the styles are different, but one thing is the same: *the heart.* And the heart is what *God* is after!

Styles of Worship Vary From Generation to Generation

Styles of worship change from generation to generation, but one generation isn't right and another generation wrong. They're just different! Whatever your age, your culture, or nation, find the style that suits you best, and worship the Lord with all your heart. What is most important is that you enter His presence with humble adoration and worship the King of kings. As you do, He will come, enthrone Himself upon your worship, and usher in His manifested glory.

If you're a little older, you may hear today's new worship songs and prefer a different style. But realize that when you were younger, it's likely an older generation said the same thing about the worship music *you* liked at the time.

In the program, Rick shared, "When the song *Onward Christian Soldiers* first came out…it was viewed to be a radical, rebellious kind of music in the church that should not be permitted — because it was *new*. It was a new style, but we grew up thinking that it was just a *wonderful* song. That's what we were accustomed to, but another generation was not accustomed to it, so they were a little put off by that."

If you grew up in a particular church, then you probably adapted to a certain kind of worship. In the Body of Christ there are Catholics, Baptists, Pentecostals, Methodists, Episcopalians, Presbyterians, Assemblies of God, and more. If you were raised in a denomination where you were accustomed to a vibrant worship style and you visit a church where the worship is more contemplative, rather than tuning out because it isn't as familiar to you, enter into worship and embrace the contrast in that style.

God Loves Variety!

In the First Century, there were different cultures in Rome, North Africa, Greece, Israel, Turkey, and other places in the Middle East. All of those cultures and the churches in them had different worship styles and sounds. And that was absolutely fine, as long as their *heart* was to worship God. There's beauty in having a variety of worship styles.

The Bible says, "Let all things be done…" (1 Corinthians 14:40). We need to do it *all* because God loves it all. He loves variety! The throne of God is filled with all kinds of beautiful colors and hues — the Bible says it's like a rainbow (*see* Revelation 4:3). God loves all kinds of variety, and that includes worship styles and sounds.

You may personally believe that praise and worship with instruments, clapping, dancing, and all kinds of celebration is the right approach to worship. Or you may be a person who loves a quieter, more reverent form of worship with hymns and organ music. You may even enjoy *both* types of worship at different times. Regardless of your preferences, there are scriptures to support your view of what worship ought to be.

Plan and Organize Worship Sets
for Worship Services

"Let all things be done decently and in order" (1 Corinthians 14:40). What does that mean? We have to go to the Greek to find out. The word "decently" is only found three places in the New Testament: Romans 13:13, First Thessalonians 4:12, and First Corinthians 14:40. In all three places it depicts *doing something honestly* or *walking honestly*, and it carries the idea of *something done properly as opposed to being done improperly*.

The word "order" in Greek is the word *taksis*, and it pictures *something done in a fitting way* or *something done according to order*. But if you look at how this word "order," was used by the Jewish historian Josephus, you'll really understand what Paul was talking about.

The Jewish historian Josephus used the Greek word *taksis* — translated "order" — when he recorded the orderly way in which the Roman army erected their camps, indicating their camps were organized and well-planned. Likewise, the word "order" indicates things should be orderly, organized, and well-planned.

This tells us Roman army commanders did not engage in last minute planning. Their camps were not hastily thrown together at the last moment; rather, they were set up in an organized and thoughtful manner. Josephus also used this word "order," the Greek word *taksis*, to describe how the Essene Jews were *respectful* of others. This particular sect of Jews would wait until others were finished speaking before they would take their turn to speak in order to show respect.

Josephus' depiction tells us that this word "order" pictures people who were *respectful, differential, courteous, accommodating, well-mannered,* and *polite*.

Taking all of this into account, here is the *Renner Interpretive Version* (*RIV*) of First Corinthians 14:40:

> **Let everything be done in a fitting and proper manner that is organized, well-planned, respectful, well-mannered, and polite.**

Notice, First Corinthians 14:40 doesn't say anything about style and it doesn't say anything about sound. Instead, the Bible talks about *intention* and *motivation* — which throws open the door to all kinds of sounds and all kinds of styles. That means worship can be quiet, or it can be loud.

Worship can be soft, or it can be bold. But worship should *not* be something just thrown together at the last moment with no thought and no organization. We're talking about worshiping Almighty God — and He deserves the very best.

Leave Room for the Holy Spirit To Move

When we plan a corporate worship service, it should be well thought out and organized prior to the service. But when we come together to worship the Lord, we also need to leave room for the Holy Spirit to change things up if He desires to, because sometimes He moves spontaneously during a service. The Holy Spirit knows the needs of everyone in the room, so it's important to follow His leading during a worship service.

It's important to be courteous and respectful of others while worshiping. But simply being quiet does not mean everything is in order. Worship doesn't have to do with volume, style, sound, or movement — it has to do with *the heart*! What you do does impact other people, so if you like to swing your arms during worship, just be sure you don't accidentally hit another person. But worship with all of your heart and remember that other people are there too.

There are also times you can be quiet and absolutely in order. It may be that God wants to talk to you during times of worship, and you have to get quiet to hear Him. Or maybe you go to a Charismatic church where you worship with volume and joy. Well, God is a joyous God! Or maybe you go to a Catholic, Presbyterian, or Episcopalian church and experience real reverence in worship. Well, the Bible says, "Be still, and know that I am God…" (Psalm 46:10). There is beauty in a variety of types of worship! There's a place for it all!

It's possible for a group of believers to be bold, loud, and yet well-mannered all at the same time. A group of believers can also be reverent, quiet, and respectful while they worship. What is your intent and heart motivation when you worship? Don't get upset if others worship a little differently than you. If you worship God from a pure heart, your worship is received by God!

Don't Just Go Through the Motions, Focus on God During Worship!

If we only go through the motions of worship, but we're simultaneously thinking about what we're going to eat or about an offense we have toward someone else — that's not worship! Going through the motions doesn't make it worship. True worship is of the heart, and you need to be focused on *God* while worshiping.

When people are outwardly expressive of their love for God and delight in Him without restraint, move out of the way, if necessary, and let them enjoy His presence. Remember King David? When he came into Jerusalem with the Ark of the Covenant, he threw off his clothes and danced all the way into the city. His wife saw him dance before the Lord, and despised it, and she was stricken barren as a result. God received David's dance as worship, but his wife judged him and suffered steep consequences as a result (*see* 2 Samuel 6:14-23).

The point is: don't get hung up on musical styles or sounds. Yes, each of us has personal preferences when it comes to worship music, but if somebody else is really worshiping God from their heart, that is between them and God. You can choose *your* expression of worship and do what is fitting that helps *you* enter into the presence of God.

God Sits Enthroned on Your Praises and in His Presence — Everything Changes!

Remember, just because somebody worships differently from you does not mean that they are not worshiping. If you travel around the United States, there may be different worship styles from California to the Deep South, and additional worship styles in the Northeast. Why? Because there are different cultures in all of those places.

It's not necessarily the sound or the style. It's *the heart* that is important. God is after the heart. And that's what we read in John 4:23 and 24, where Jesus said, "But the hour cometh, and now is, when the true worshippers shall worship the Father in spirit and in truth: for the Father seeketh such to worship him. God is a Spirit: and they that worship him must worship him in spirit and in truth." If you worship in spirit and in truth, then you will form a channel, or a conduit, which brings God's powerful presence right to where you are and shifts everything in your life.

The word "worship" is the Greek word *proskuneo*, a compound of the word *pros* — which means *to draw near* — and the word *kuneo* — which means *to kiss*. When you combine the two words together, it means *to draw near and to blow intimate kisses in worship*. That's intimacy.

God wants to invade your world, and He sits enthroned upon your praises. When you worship Him, He says, "I like it so much, I'm going to go down there and join them." And He comes with His powerful presence. When God's presence shows up, *everything* begins to change. If there's anything crooked, it's going to be made straight; if there's anything lame, it's going to be healed. That's what happens when God's powerful presence shows up!

STUDY QUESTIONS

Study to shew thyself approved unto God, a workman that needeth not to be ashamed, rightly dividing the word of truth.
— 2 Timothy 2:15

1. Notice it didn't take extravagant instrumentation and perfected vocal arrangements to bring the presence of God on the scene when Paul and Silas were unjustly imprisoned (*see* Acts 16:25), or when John was exiled and living in a cave (*see* Revelation 1:9,10). With sincere hearts, Paul, Silas, and John drew near to God, and as an act of faith, they magnified Him rather than magnifying the circumstances that surrounded them. What are you magnifying? The problem, or the Father?

2. Psalm 24:3 and 4 talks about coming before the Lord with clean hands and a pure heart. Examine your heart in order to prepare for your time of worship at home alone or at church. If there is anything you need to repent of before entering into worship, come before the Lord and ask for His forgiveness. Consider Psalm 51:10, First John 1:9, and Psalm 119:9.

3. Hebrews 13:15 says, "By him therefore let us offer the sacrifice of praise to God continually, that is, the fruit of our lips giving thanks to his name." When Paul and Silas worshiped God from prison, God's manifested presence was drawn to their sacrifice of praise. His delivering and saving power came and shook the very foundations of the prison. What would have happened if Paul and Silas *didn't* praise God in their midnight hour? What will you do in your midnight hour? How will your decision to worship God impact the situation?

PRACTICAL APPLICATION

But be ye doers of the word, and not hearers only,
deceiving your own selves.
— James 1:22

1. When it comes to your relationship with Jesus, if you're not on fire spiritually like you were in the past, it's not too late to return to your First Love with all of your heart (*see* Revelation 2:4). Stir up the embers of your love for Him. How? Praise God for His great love for you displayed in Jesus! Remember how He sought you out and the beauty of receiving Him into your heart. He loves you, and He is waiting with open arms to make all things new again (*see* John 3:16,17; Romans 8:1; Psalm 51:12; and 2 Corinthians 5:17).

2. Read Romans 4:20. Notice how Abraham praised God by faith rather than considering the fact that he and his wife Sarah were too old to have children. Giving glory to God is an act of faith in the face of what looks impossible. Consider Luke 1:37, Luke 18:27, and Romans 4:17-21. What is it that looks impossible in your life? Take time now to praise God for making the impossible possible. He is God! Have faith in the faithful One — God!

The title of this series is *Encountering God's Powerful Presence in Worship*. When was the last time you truly *encountered* God's presence? What happened as a result? Meditate on James 4:8 and Jeremiah 31:3. Draw near to Him and receive His love as you encounter His powerful presence in worship today!

Notes

CLAIM YOUR FREE RESOURCE!

As a way of introducing you further to the teaching ministry of Rick Renner, we would like to send you free of charge his teaching CD, "How To Receive a Miraculous Touch From God."

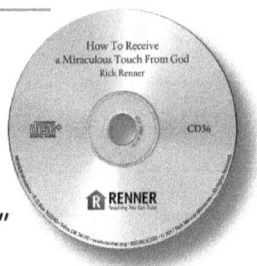

In His earthly ministry, Jesus commonly healed *all* who were sick of *all* their diseases. In this profound message, learn about the manifold dimensions of Christ's wisdom, goodness, power, and love toward all humanity who came to Him in faith with their needs.

☑ YES, I want to receive Rick Renner's monthly teaching letter!

Simply scan the QR code to claim this resource or go to: **renner.org/claim-your-free-offer**

Connect

WITH US!